Amazing OTTERS

A sea otter is ready to break open a clamshell on a rock that rests on its belly.

by M. Barbara Brownell

■ BOOKS FOR YOUNG EXPLORERS
NATIONAL GEOGRAPHIC SOCIETY

Three sea otters rock gently
in the water. They lie wrapped
in giant seaweed called kelp.
Otters roll and play and even
rest among the plants.

Sea otters often float together
in groups called rafts. You can
see rafts of otters off the coasts
of California and Alaska.

Not all sea otters look alike.
An old male otter often has white
fur. Even two otters with dark fur
look different when one is wet
and the other is dry.

An otter's eyes and nose are high up
on its head. It can easily see and
breathe as it swims at the surface.
An otter's whiskers help it feel
its way in muddy water.

For an otter, anytime can be playtime. One minute, it may be relaxing with its feet up. The next minute, it may roll over on its stomach and dive. The otter will kick its big feet, which are webbed like a duck's, and glide underwater. There, it may play tag with another otter. Sometimes otters turn somersaults.

As she floats, a sea otter mother holds her baby tightly. The baby is called a pup. Most of the time, sea otters give birth in the water in a bed of kelp.

Waves moving the kelp up and down rock the pup to sleep.
Some people call the kelp "a sea otter's cradle."
You can almost hear this mother hum "Rock-a-bye, Baby."

Lying on top of its mother, a pup drinks her milk. Pups can be born in any season. A sea otter raises only one at a time. A newborn otter is tiny and almost helpless. In a few weeks, it learns to swim. Later, it learns to find its own food.

The mother watches over her pup for six months or more. If a strange otter comes near, the mother snorts a warning. She swims to her pup and stays until the other otter leaves.

With a splash, an otter bangs a clam against a rock it put on its belly. When the shell cracks open, the otter will eat the soft clam inside. Then it will roll over and wash itself in the water. An otter needs to eat a lot each day!

A sea otter often carries a favorite rock wherever it goes, even when it dives for sea urchins. A sea urchin has sharp, pointed spines. The otter is able to eat it without getting hurt because the otter's mouth has tough skin.

In its bed of kelp, an otter
twists around to rub its fur
with a paw. It is spreading air
bubbles through the fur.
The bubbles help make
the coat waterproof and
keep the otter comfortable
in the water all year around.

Many sea otters float in kelp
both day and night.
Kelp grows up from the
seafloor. Under the water,
the kelp is like a forest.
There, otters find food.

A sea otter takes a nap in the cold water. Its thick fur is like a waterproof blanket that has two layers. The top coat has longer hair. Bubbles of air, trapped in the shorter underfur, help keep the otter warm and dry.

Sea otters have cousins called river otters. This kind of
river otter lives in Asia. River otters live in almost every
part of the world. They don't stay in the water as much as
sea otters do. They fish and play in rivers and streams.
Then they go onto land and curl up in homes called dens.

Two river otters in India stand
up on their hind legs. Otters
sometimes hold themselves up
with their tails.

The largest of all river otters
is the giant Brazilian otter.
It can be five feet or longer
from head to tail.

Two giant otters and a caiman watch each other carefully.
What do you think will happen? Probably nothing.
Otters and caimans usually hunt in the water, anyway.

If the caiman attacked them, the otters could easily
defend themselves. They have strong jaws and sharp teeth.
These otters would probably help each other in a fight.

21

It's time for a sunbath!
After a swim, a river otter
goes on land to dry off and
to rest. It finds a sunny spot
hidden by reeds or bushes.

Sometimes an otter sits
by the water. It stays alert,
sniffing the air for danger.

An otter zooms along underwater,
pushing with its webbed feet.
The tail helps it steer.

This otter is fishing by a
beaver lodge. Sometimes a female
uses an empty beaver lodge as
a den. She gives birth there,
on a bed of dry twigs and grasses.
A river otter has two to six babies.

When a river otter is hungry, it may
go hunting along the edge of the
water. Sometimes it catches a mouse.
It may even find a tasty fish.
A river otter uses its sharp teeth
to eat a whole fish—even the bones!

Later, the otter may dive in and
grab an eel—one of its favorite snacks.
Like sea otters, river otters wash
themselves in the water after a meal.

On a frozen pond, an otter pokes its head into a hole
in the ice. The otter goes in deeper and deeper. Kerplunk!
It dives in. In a few minutes, it comes up for a breath
of air. River otters love swimming in cold water.
Like sea otters, they have thick fur to keep them warm.

An otter races through the snow, then plops down
and glides. A frozen lake makes a good playground
for river otters. Sledding down the bank and sliding
across the lake, otters leave a trail in the snow.
Just like sea otters, river otters like having fun.

A sea otter clutches its food tightly as seagulls come near. The birds often drop in to snatch a free meal when otters are eating.

COVER: Two river otters cuddle after playing. Otters like to touch each other.

Published by

The National Geographic Society, Washington, D. C.
Gilbert M. Grosvenor, *President and Chairman of the Board*
Melvin M. Payne, Thomas W. McKnew, *Chairmen Emeritus*
Owen R. Anderson, *Executive Vice President*
Robert L. Breeden, *Senior Vice President,*
    Publications and Educational Media

Prepared by

The Special Publications and School Services Division
Donald J. Crump, *Director*
Philip B. Silcott, *Associate Director*
Bonnie S. Lawrence, *Assistant Director*

Staff for this book

Jane H. Buxton, *Managing Editor*
Charles E. Herron, *Illustrations Editor*
Viviane Y. Silverman, *Art Director*
Ann Nottingham Kelsall, *Researcher*
Artemis S. Lampathakis, *Illustrations Assistant*
Susan A. Bender, Catherine G. Cruz, Marisa J.
    Farabelli, Lisa A. LaFuria, Sandra F. Lotterman,
    Eliza C. Morton, Dru McLoud Stancampiano,
    Staff Assistants

Engraving, Printing, and Product Manufacture

George V. White, *Director,* and Vincent P. Ryan,
    Manager, Manufacturing and Quality Management
David V. Showers, *Production Manager*
Kathleen M. Cirucci, *Production Project Manager*
Carol R. Curtis, *Senior Production Staff Assistant*

Consultants

Dr. Nicole Duplaix, GeoServices, Inc., Boynton
    Beach, Florida, and Dr. James A. Estes, Institute
    of Marine Sciences, University of California at
    Santa Cruz, Santa Cruz, California, *Scientific*
    Consultants
Dr. Ine N. Noe, *Educational Consultant*
Dr. Lynda Bush, *Reading Consultant*

Illustrations Credits

James R. Fisher/National Audubon Society Collection/PR (cover); Tom and Pat Leeson (1, 6 upper left, 13, 24-25); Frans Lanting (2-3, 4); John Gerlach/DRK Photo (3); Richard A. Bucich (5 both); James A. Mattison, Jr., MD. (6-7); Lon E. Lauber (8-9, 11 lower left and right); Lon E. Lauber/West Stock (10-11); Jeff Foott (12); Jeff Foott/DRK Photo (14-15); Kennan Ward (16-17); Nancy Adams/Tom Stack & Associates (18); S. Nagendra/National Audubon Society Collection/PR (19 upper); National Geographic Photographer Bates Littlehales (19 lower); Warren Garst/Tom Stack & Associates (20-21); Alan and Sandy Carey (22-23, 31, 32); Animals Animals/Stouffer Productions Ltd. (24); C. C. Lockwood (26-27); Animals Animals/Len Rue, Jr. (27); Len Rue, Jr. (28-29, 29 upper); E.P.I. Nancy Adams (29 lower); Jess R. Lee (30 all).

Library of Congress ℭℑℙ Data
Brownell, M. Barbara.
    Amazing otters / by M. Barbara Brownell.
    p.   cm. — (Books for young explorers)
    Bibliography: p.
    Summary: Introduces in text and illustrations, the physical characteristics, habits, and natural environment of the otter.
    ISBN 0–87044–770–X : (regular edition) — ISBN 0–87044–775–0 (library edition)
    1. Otters—Juvenile literature.   [1. Otters.]   I. Title.
II. Series.
QL737.C25B76   1989
599.74′447—dc20   89-3278
                                                        ℭℑℙ
                                                         AC

MORE ABOUT Amazing Otters

"Let's play!" If an otter could talk, this might be its favorite expression. This long, sleek mammal is a juggler, acrobat, and prankster. An otter may shoot out of the water, nip a beaver's tail, then disappear again. It may juggle shells or stones with its agile paws.

Biologists classify otters as Mustelidae. This large family of mammals includes weasels, skunks, and martens, among others. Of the many species of otters, most live in fresh water—rivers, lakes, and streams—the world over.

Only a few species are found along seacoasts. One, *Enhydra lutris*, is commonly called the sea otter. Sea otters spend most of their lives in the water, but they may go ashore at times. They live along the northern Pacific coasts of North America and parts of Asia. Another marine species inhabits Pacific coastal waters of South America.

The freshwater species, often referred to as river otters, spend much of their time on land. For shelter, they usually dig a burrow, or holt, into a riverbank, often with one entrance above the water and one below. Or they may move into a hollow tree trunk or other ready-made nesting place. Their home range may extend 10 to 12 miles along a bank. Like other members of the family Mustelidae, the river otter marks its range with a smelly liquid from glands near its tail.

Despite differences in habitats, all otters have similar body structures. The body is streamlined, with a powerful tapered tail. The legs are short and the head is broad and slightly flat. The spine is so flexible that an otter can bend itself nose to tail tip in either direction (6-7).*

Sea otters are generally heavier than river otters. An average adult sea otter measures between 4 and 5 feet from its head to the tip of its tail and weighs about 60 pounds. The different species of river otters vary greatly in length and weight. Giant Brazilian otters (20-21) rival

* Numbers in parentheses refer to pages in *Amazing Otters*.

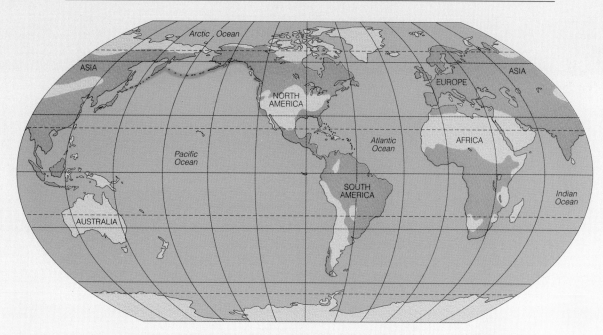

Range of River Otters ■   *Range of Sea Otters in this Book* ■

Otters live on all continents except Australia and Antarctica. They are not found in desert or polar regions. Sea otters live mainly along the Pacific coast of North and South America; river otters inhabit rivers and streams in many places.

even the largest sea otters in length, but they are not as heavy.

Rich, silky fur covers all otters. The densest of any mammal's, the otter's coat has up to 850,000 hair follicles per square inch. Otters have two layers of fur—and little fat. As an otter leaps in and out of the water, air bubbles build up between the layers of fur, forming a cushion that holds in body heat. An otter uses its teeth to comb its fur to help get rid of tangles and to fluff up the underfur.

To keep its coat water resistant, an otter grooms, or preens, constantly (14-15). Using its teeth, tongue, claws, a rock, a shell, or a piece of kelp, an otter combs out any dirt or food residue. Preening is a key to survival. If the fur is dirty, it will lose its water resistance, and the otter can die of exposure. The young learn to preen even before they learn to find food.

Otters eat a lot of food. They must burn many calories to stay warm. An otter may spend half its waking hours hunting and eating. Most otters like eels. River otters may catch fish, mice, and other small animals (26-27). Sea otters eat sea urchins (12), abalone, and clams, which abound in kelp beds.

The sea otter is one of the few mammals that use tools. To dine on shellfish it brings up from the seafloor, an otter floats on its back. It places on its belly a rock, also from the seafloor, and smacks the shellfish against it, cracking open the shell (1, 13). Sometimes an otter has a favorite rock that it carries in a fold of skin under its arm.

As an otter dives, its ears and nostrils clamp shut, keeping out water. Its eyes stay open (24); the otter sees as well underwater as it does above. Large lung capacity enables an otter to stay under for four minutes and swim a quarter of a mile.

BRIAN MILNE/FIRST LIGHT

Thicker than any other mammal's, an otter's fur clings in spikes when wet.

Otters often float on their backs with their feet out of the water (2-3, 6). The feet have little fur. Scientists believe that keeping them dry helps otters conserve body heat.

Otters are curious about their surroundings, and they seem to have a lot to say about what they see. Unlike other Mustelidae, otters do a lot of chattering. Sea otters playing might squawk like seagulls, as if to say, "Don't be a bully!" "Hah?" is a universal challenge (11) to intruders, "Who are you?"

Touching is another way otters communicate (cover, 6-7). Mothers spend a lot of time preening and cuddling their young (8-9, 10-11), reinforcing the close bond between them. Mother otters usually raise the pups without assistance from the fathers. A sea otter gives birth in the water or along the shore. Almost always, she has only one pup. A river otter, on the other hand, may bear as many as six pups in her den, but usually no more than four live to maturity.

Violent storms present a great danger to otters. The animals are thrown against the rocks and may drown or die of exposure if they cannot feed or preen properly. Humans have been a different kind of enemy. In 1741, a Russian expedition discovered sea otters along northern Pacific coasts and found that the animals' warm, soft pelts brought high prices. Soon, hunters from many countries came looking for otter pelts. By the early 1900s, sea otters were nearly extinct.

Since 1911, governments and conservationists the world over have been trying to save them. Otters are protected by law in some places, and their numbers are slowly rising. Still they are not safe. Sea otters are often strangled in fishermen's nets, or poisoned by oil spills. A major spill off Alaska's coast in March 1989 killed many of them. Of the river otters, the giant Brazilian otter is the most endangered.

If you travel along the coast of California, you can visit places where sea otters thrive. Most other kinds of otters are shy and hard to find outside of zoos. Walking along a riverbank, you might find footprints, mud slides, or nests that tell you that otters have been there; but you are not likely to get more than a glance at the animals in the wild.

Additional Reading

A Raft of Sea Otters, by Vicki Leon. (San Luis Obispo, CA, Blake Publishing, 1987). Ages 6-12.

Amazing Animals of the Sea, by Catherine O'Neill and Judith E. Rinard. (Washington, D. C., National Geographic Society, 1981). Ages 8 -12.

Book of Mammals, 2 vols. (Washington, D. C., National Geographic Society, 1981). Ages 8 and up.